To

_____

From

_____

Date

_____

When Someone You Love Has Cancer

Comfort and Encouragement
for Caregivers and Loved Ones

Cecil Murphey

Illustrated by *Michal Sparks*

HARVEST HOUSE PUBLISHERS

EUGENE, OREGON

When Someone You Love Has Cancer

Text Copyright © 2009 by Cecil Murphey
Art Copyright by Michal Sparks

Published by Harvest House Publishers
Eugene, Oregon 97402
www.harvesthousepublishers.com

ISBN 978-0-7369-2428-3

Design and production by Garborg Design Works, Savage, Minnesota

Scripture verses are taken from the *Holy Bible*, New Living Translation, copyright ©1996, 2004. Used by permission of Tyndale House Publishers, Inc., Wheaton, IL 60189 USA. All rights reserved.

For Shirley

I loved you before the cancer.

Each morning I thank

God for giving us

one more day together

on this earth.

Contents

Introduction

I felt helpless.

Shirley, the person I loved most in the world, had been diagnosed with breast cancer. She was in the high-risk category.

As her husband, I couldn't make her better or take away the diagnosis. I felt powerless and empty. I did for her the only thing I could—and I did it for me as well—I prayed.

We are the blessed ones because Shirley survived and remains symptom free a decade later.

Whatever the results, one thing we learned: God was with us and strengthened us both through the many weeks of uncertainty and pain.

May God sustain you through the cancer journey.

1

"I Just Need a Little Reassurance"

The doctor walked into the room, and his shoulders slumped. First he stared at her, then at the walls, and finally at his feet. "I have bad news for you." He paused, started to make eye contact, but then looked away. "I'm sorry," he said. "The biopsy...cancer..."

We listened, although we didn't absorb much information after the doctor said the word we hadn't wanted to hear.

Even before the tests, I think she knew. But she hadn't been able to say the word, at least not out loud. Even though the doctor said something such as, "This probably isn't terminal. We think we've caught it in time," she still focused on the dreaded word.

"How long do I have?" my friend asked.

"I can't answer that. We hope we can cure this." He spoke again about treatment and things they would do. Part of his explanation seemed to come out of his nervousness. As he talked I watched her eyes, and it was obvious she was no longer listening to what he said.

At this stage I only
wanted to comfort
and encourage her.
This wasn't the time to
confront and challenge.

She was looking into the future and didn't see much ahead for herself.

As soon as we walked outside the doctor's office, my friend asked, "Why me?" Before I could respond, she said, "Have I failed God? Is this some kind of punishment?"

"I don't know," was my answer then. It's my answer now.

Maybe that's part of the agony most people go through. It's as if they need to discover a reason. They want an explanation as to why this terrible disease has touched them.

I don't say it, but I think, *Even if an answer were possible, would it change anything*?

The perplexing questions continued to come from her lips as we got into the car. "Why? Why me? Why now?"

Just before we reached her house, she slammed her fist against the car door. "Why would God do this to me? If God truly loved me, then I wouldn't have this...this disease."

She still wasn't ready to say the name of the disease. In time I knew she would. Eventually, it would become a significant word she would repeat a dozen times a day. But for the moment, "cancer" wasn't a word in her personal vocabulary. Her mind wasn't ready to accept the reality. At this stage I only wanted to comfort and encourage her. This wasn't the time to confront and challenge.

As I listened to my friend's voice and sensed the stress she was going through, I wished I could do something for her, something to make her feel better. But then, I realized, I was really more concerned about myself. I wanted to feel better. I hated the discomfort I was going through. I wanted to take away the diagnosis or say, "It's really nothing."

Yet it *was* something—something big and significant—and her life would never be the same again.

A doctor once told me that often the first spoken words after patients hear their diagnosis of any serious disease are often words of anger or blame directed at God. This was the first time I had witnessed someone's reaction.

Another set of questions turns the focus inward:

- Is *it because of something* I *did wrong or didn't do right*?
- Is *it because* I've *allowed sinful thoughts to control my mind*?
- Have I *disobeyed God*?
- Should I *have done more for other people*?
- Am I *holding a grudge against anyone*?

Another friend diagnosed with breast cancer had been part of a blind study on hormone replacement. She asked, "Did that cause my cancer?" (Her doctor explained that the cancer had existed before the study began.)

11

Even though patients ask unanswerable questions, they don't expect us to explain. When my friend kept asking, "Why? Why me?" I didn't try to find logical answers. I wouldn't have known what to say.

I didn't answer because I believed there were stronger, more compelling questions she needed answered:

- *Do you care—really care—about me?*
- *Does God love me?*
- *Will my family and friends hover around me as I go through my treatment?*
- *Will you love me even if I'm disfigured or feel unattractive?*

I wasn't the only person who cared. I was a friend. She also had family members. She had the family of the church and others on whom to rely.

Most important, she had God. Sometimes, however, it's hard for people to think about God's love or sense the divine presence. That's when they need people like you and me to be present and to assure them that God's love is as strong now as it has ever been.

I took my friend's hand and said softly, "I love you. I promise to pray for you every day while you're going through this."

At first she said nothing, but her eyes told me she grasped the meaning I wanted to convey. She smiled and then said, "I know. I just need a little reassurance right now."

God of all Power and Wisdom, I don't know why my friend has cancer, and I'm not asking you to explain. I am asking you to assure her of your abiding love. Assure me of your presence as I try to be available for her.

Amen.

2

Talking About It

"I don't want to talk about it," she said.

"It's all right," I said. "When you're ready to talk, I'm ready to listen."

She wasn't trying to shut me out, but she wasn't trying to bring me into her private world, either. She wasn't even thinking about me. I had been beside her when the doctor said the word "cancer." I don't know how much more she heard.

The word can be frightening. Years ago John Wayne did a commercial and referred to his lung cancer as "the big C." Although he was reading a script, whoever wrote the words probably understood how difficult it is for some people to name the disease. "Big C" is one way not to speak about the reality of the situation. It's a temporary form of denial.

For many, to say the word is to claim the diagnosis, and she wasn't

ready to accept what she had heard. I understood. Even though the doctor assured her that her chances of surviving were good, even high, she wasn't ready to hear even that much. A diagnosis—a serious diagnosis—is almost always a moment of deep psychological distress and spiritual crisis.

"I've never faced a more daunting challenge in my life," one of her friends said.

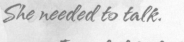

She needed to talk.

I needed to listen.

"Though I survived, I couldn't think about survival in the beginning. I could only think that my life would never be the same again."

Days went by, and my friend said nothing about the diagnosis. At lunch a week later, she finally said, "I've been through a lot in my life." She referred to a divorce, financial problems, the shifting job market, and problems with her older son. "But nothing else was quite like this. They all seem suddenly insignificant."

I resisted the urge to tell her she would feel better or that she was thinking negatively. She needed to talk. I needed to listen.

It was as if she had been mentally paralyzed for seven days and now she was ready to move slowly out of the fear that froze her feelings. "The doctor said, 'I'm sorry, but the biopsy indicates that it's cancer. We'll have to do further tests to know how serious.' Nothing made sense after that. His mouth moved and words came out. I heard what he said, but he might as well have been speaking Swahili. My mind went blank. I wanted to leave his office and get away from everyone."

I knew enough about cancer patients to realize her reaction wasn't unusual, especially when the patient hadn't expected to hear that diagnosis.

I touched her hand. If she wanted to talk more, she could. Or we could sit in silence. She chose the latter for perhaps ten minutes before she said, "You know what I was the most afraid of?" Before I could answer, she said, "The pain. I just didn't want to hurt, and I didn't want to lie uselessly for weeks in a bed."

She stopped talking and didn't mention the subject for several days. When she was ready, she said, "I suppose you think I'm some kind of crybaby."

"No, I think you're facing a serious illness. You reacted the way that's the most natural for you."

At first, I'm not sure she grasped what I meant. All of us respond to stress in individual ways. Doctors tell me that some people sit calmly and discuss the seriousness of a malignancy as if it meant having to have a wart removed.

Some demand statistics. "What are my chances of recovery?" When they hear, for example, that it's 90 percent treatable, some patients smile and feel encouraged. Others say, "But ten out of every hundred die. Is that what you mean?"

I've heard of patients who burst into tears and cry for three minutes or three hours. Once they have emptied

All of us respond to stress in individual ways.

19

Just giving her permission to talk, or not to talk, may be the most healing thing I can do for her.

themselves of tears, it's as if they have put the issues behind them and are ready for whatever they have to face.

All this means there is a right way to respond to the news—and she responded in exactly the right way. She did what was natural and appropriate for her.

Because I love her, I want her to be herself, to respond emotionally in the way that works best for her. If I try to push her into what I consider the healthier way of facing her cancer, I may be doing her great harm.

If I listen, if I care, if I reach out in compassion, I can do her no harm. Just giving her permission to talk, or not to talk, may be the most healing thing I can do for her.

God of All Love and Grace, thank you that you've made each of us differently. The psalmist says we are fearfully and wonderfully made, and my friend's reaction helps me understand her better. It also helps me to better understand your love and compassion for us. Thank you.

Amen.

3

What Can I Do for Him?

I wanted to help him, but I didn't know what to do, so I held back. He was undergoing chemo treatments before I finally got involved.

I knew I had been wrong to wait. Part of the reason was not knowing what to do, but there was also something else—something quite selfish. Reaching out to a friend was going to upset my normal routine. Yes, that was selfish of me, but that's who I was. I never said the words to anyone, but it hadn't been convenient for me to help.

One day when I was praying, I felt guilty over my attitude. As I prayed, the thought came to me that it wasn't convenient for him to have cancer. That same day I called and asked, "May I come and see you?"

I was too embarrassed to tell him why I hadn't been previously involved, but I let him know I was there today. "I want to be available to you whenever I can or for whatever you need."

He stared at me for a long time before he said, "I don't want you to *do* anything. I have people who provide for the *things* I need." He paused and leaned forward. "I'll tell you what I want from you. I just want you to be available when I need to talk. Just that."

Just that. I seemed to have so little to offer, but he wasn't concerned about little or much. He wanted my presence, my availability. More than I had realized, perhaps he understood why I hadn't been there before.

"I'm available. Anytime." And as I said those words I meant them.

He took me up on my offer. After that, he called me three or four times a week. He only wanted me to be there for him. He didn't want

3 Ways to Care

• *Be available*

• *Be supportive*

• *Listen*

my advice, my medical information, or my theological explanations. He wanted me.

A second thing I did for him was to be supportive. Perhaps that's part of being available, but I saw them as two separate things. Being available meant my willingness to be present by his bedside or on the phone. Being supportive meant I encouraged him.

One day, for instance, he had a bad day. I could see depression written across his face when I came into his bedroom.

"You're having a rough day, aren't you?"

He nodded.

"The doctor said you'd have bad days, and this is one of them. Every day won't be like today. I'm here while you go through this bad day."

Did he know that? Of course he did, but when I spoke, light slowly came into his eyes. He smiled.

My words didn't make the difference, but my attitude did. Because I came with a spirit of encouragement, he responded.

Here's the third thing I learned: I listened. When he spoke, I knew exactly what to say to make him feel better, and I could have given answers to many of the questions he asked. But I said nothing, and that was the right response.

I nodded. I smiled. I frowned. But I kept my mouth shut. I learned to listen in silence. My friend didn't need information, even if he had asked. He needed to know I was comfortable just being with him.

The best time of all I had during the months of his recovery was the day I sat beside him and neither of us spoke for perhaps ten minutes.

When I finally stood to leave, he clasped my hand and said, "You are a special friend."

My friend's cancer is now in remission, but it was a slow, agonizing process. I tried to be there and encourage him. The most valuable lesson I learned in the process was that I didn't need to wait to be asked. He needed my presence and my encouragement. He needed me to listen. I regret that it took me so long to figure that out.

Great God of Silence and Peace, thank you that I can do so much for a hurting friend even though it seems to be so little. Remind me that my presence is more important than my actions.

Amen.

4

"No One Understands"

"How do you feel?" I asked.

"I hurt." For several minutes she talked about her pain since the surgery as if no one else in the world had ever hurt before. I almost said, "You're not the first person in the universe to have cancer." I stopped myself as I thought, *That's true, but this is the first time in the universe she has had cancer.*

I didn't know how she felt. I didn't understand—how could I? But I cared and I tried to express my concern.

While I sat next to her, a member of her Sunday school class came to visit.

They chatted a few minutes, and then the visitor said, "My dear, I know exactly how you feel."

I didn't interrupt, but after the visitor left, she grumbled, "She has

I don't want to be patronized or to be given the right words without the right feelings.

no idea how much I hurt."

"That's true," I said. "How could anyone else know exactly how much pain you feel?" I paused before I added, "I don't know how you feel. I've never had cancer. I've never had pain like that."

Her eyes brimmed with tears. "You do understand then, don't you?"

I shrugged. "I'm not sure I do."

"You realize that you don't know. That's what I mean. You can't feel my pain and don't know how much I hate being in a bed, unable to take care of my house, plant my garden, and be with my friends."

"I hear what you're saying, and that's true, I can't feel the frustration and the ordeal you're going through." I took her hand in mine and said, "I love you. I don't really understand, but I'm here for you."

"That's what I meant," she said. "You don't understand, and as crazy as it sounds, that is understanding. That may not make sense to you, but you don't try to tell me you can feel my pain or my frustration. You can't know the things I worry about, but you're here. You don't run away when I talk about those things."

"I want to be here whenever you need me."

"That's what I meant about people not understanding. They get

I would try to understand from my heart and not from my mind, experience, or stored-up knowledge.

uncomfortable when I tell them how much I'm hurting, about the pain pills every four hours, or about my anger over being confined to bed for another week. They're always thinking about themselves. Maybe that's the way it is with all of us. I know I'm thinking about myself, but while I'm recovering from surgery, I don't want to be patronized or to be given the right words without the right feelings."

I smiled at her because she felt I "understood." Perhaps I did. But I also thought about other times, other friends, and other situations. I hadn't cared as deeply or hadn't been as close to the hurting person as I could have been. This time it was different.

As I sat beside her, I silently prayed that from now on, every time would be different. I would try to understand from my heart and not from my mind, experience, or stored-up knowledge. If I responded from who I was—from my emotions and my soul—I didn't have to worry about whether I understood. I needed only to care. If I cared, that was what she needed most. Caring may not be the same as understanding, but it is the closest I can come.

All-Wise and All-Knowing God, no matter how hard I try, I never fully understand anyone else. I don't even understand myself. But I can care for those who are going through difficult times. Strengthen me to reach out to those who hurt, even if I can't feel their pain as they do.

Amen.

5

"What Kind of Wife Am I?"

One day she reached the end of her patience. She yelled at him. She felt guilty—but only briefly. She apologized. A few days later she became upset and failed him again.

"What kind of wife am I?" she wailed to God. "How can I have these terrible moments of impatience? He's sick and I'm the one with the problem."

She didn't get an answer that day, but over the next few months as his inoperable cancer grew, she learned many things.

First, she admitted that she had tried to be Superwoman. She assumed she could take care of him, handle the chores at the house, be a mother, and carry any load that fell on her shoulders.

She was wrong.

She had set herself up to fail. Worse, she tried to do it alone. Most

of the time she refused help from well-meaning friends.

She also realized that her anger covered something much, much deeper: She was afraid. She was afraid of losing him, and yet she knew she would. Except for a miracle, it was only a question of time. She was afraid of facing his death and afraid of living without him. She expressed it by being peevish or irritated. A few times she yelled at him. Afterward, she felt consumed by guilt and was in tears. "How could I possibly have shouted at him when he was sick?" she wailed. "God, what kind of loving wife am I?"

In time she realized what kind of wife she is: a very human, loving wife trying to cope with human, abnormal conditions. Yes, she failed and she'll probably fail again. But she's doing her best, and each day she reminds herself of these words, "I can do everything through Christ, who gives me strength" (Philippians 4:13).

Dear All-Perfect God, please help me to accept what I can do and relax and release the things I can't handle. When fear clutches at me, remind me of your presence and that your help is always, always there for me.

Amen.

6

Anxious and Apprehensive

Anxiety isn't the same as anger. Anger is generally directed to something specific—a person or a situation. Anxiety is apprehension. I can't usually define a specific danger or threat, but I have an overall feeling that it is not directed toward a specific cause.

Generally anxiety comes and goes quickly, but it can become so powerful it hinders me from enjoying my life each day. That's especially true when a person I love has cancer.

Anxiety is common with people like us who care for those with cancer. The way I found to deal with it was to examine it. What was making me feel anxious? The more I asked God to help me face my anxieties, the less power they held over me.

It helped me to realize that caregivers experience anxiety as much as those with cancer. And some individuals are more susceptible than others.

One caregiver said, "If I could pin down my apprehension, maybe I could do something about it. It's a vague, undefined cloud of darkness that seems to engulf me."

"Don't try to make yourself less anxious," I said. "Let God do that." After a lengthy talk I suggested verses to her and asked her to write them

down or memorize them. "Repeat these three verses each day and see if they make a difference."

- "I will not be afraid [substitute anxious], for you are close beside me. Your rod and your staff protect and comfort me" (Psalm 23:4).
- "You will keep in perfect peace all who trust in you, all whose thoughts are fixed on you!" (Isaiah 26:3).
- [Jesus said,] "Don't let your hearts be troubled. Trust in God, and trust also in me" (John 14:1).

I didn't give her a magic formula. Such a thing doesn't exist. Instead, I gave her practical ways to direct her thoughts.

She later admitted to me that when her mind focused on those verses, she was at peace. When feelings of anxiety and apprehension crept around her, she learned to quietly stop whatever she was doing and read or recite each of those verses until peace filled her heart. It wasn't a magic formula. Maybe it was just a miracle—a divine miracle God provides for those whom he loves.

God of Tranquility, help me when I grow fretful. Remind me that you are with me. Remind me that I can find peace and calmness in my soul as I open myself to you.

Amen.

7

Silence, Only Silence

"I love God, and I pray and I pray," she said, "but I receive nothing from God but silence." She told me her husband had battled colon cancer for more than a year. The doctor had given him a somewhat optimistic picture, but he still feared the future.

"I think he's going to die," she said. "That's why God isn't talking to us."

In the past I had tried any number of ways to assure her that God was with her—even in the midst of silence. Nothing happened. I prayed for guidance before I visited the next time. I listened to her moan about the heavenly lack of communication. Then I gave her my own form of shock treatment—even though I hadn't planned to say what I did.

"Is that how it works?" I asked. "When God is through with people like your husband, he tosses him aside and stops talking? He's of no value to God and neither are you."

"God isn't like that! He loves me. He loves my husband—" my friend stopped speaking suddenly and just stared at me. Then she laughed before she said, "I asked for that response, didn't I?"

For once I didn't answer, but I did smile.

"I've focused so much on what I don't know—what the future holds. Every day I worry he'll need surgery again. I worry about whether we have

enough insurance coverage and about whether he'll be able to go back to work." She went through a list of things she worried about.

"Is it possible that God can't get through to you?" I asked in a soft voice. "Is it possible that you have so many worries and anxieties filling your mind that you haven't left any space for him?"

"Probably," was her answer.

On my computer I copied two verses from the Psalms and made them into small cards so she could place them in the kitchen, the bathroom, the den, and the bedroom. "Read this whenever you face God's silence." Here is what I gave her: "When I am afraid, I will put my trust in you. I praise God for what he has promised. I trust in God, so why should I be afraid?" (Psalm 56:3-4).

Several weeks later she called me on the phone with great excitement in her voice. "Listen to these words from Philippians 4:6! I read them in my quiet time this morning. 'Don't worry about anything; instead, pray about everything. Tell God what you need, and thank him for all he has done.'"

"And the silence?" I asked.

"You were right," she said. "I let so many things crowd into my head and heart that there was no room for the Lord to speak." Before she hung up, she said, "I'm at peace. I still don't hear words from God, but I know he listens to my words."

God of All Grace, please forgive anxiety-ridden caregivers. They have so much going on, and they feel stressed on many fronts. Enable them to push unhealthy thoughts aside so they can hear from you.

Amen.

8

"God Doesn't Make Ugly"

Janet had been through four chemo treatments. She lost her hair after the first injection. It came out by the handfuls. She knelt in the shower and clasped the wet strands of hair and cried for a long time. She knew it was something that just about everyone goes through. "But I hadn't gone through it before," she said.

"I feel so ugly," Janet said to her husband and to her good friends. She hated to wear a wig because it made her feel hot and uncomfortable, so she refused to go out in public. "I look awful and I don't want anyone to see me." She lost weight. Her skin was pasty, and the dark circles under her eyes made her look as if she hadn't slept in some time.

Her friends listened to her. She had always been an attractive woman, and when she faced breast cancer, it was quite a blow to her.

"You are more than your hair, more than your figure and complexion," a friend said to her. "What you are on the inside is more important than what you are on the outside."

"I love you for who you are," her husband said. "How you look isn't everything."

"I'm a person God created out of love.
What I look like isn't nearly as important as who I am."

It took Janet a couple of weeks to get the message, but she finally said to her friends, "I'm more than my body." She smiled and said, "I'm a person God created out of love. What I look like isn't nearly as important as who I am."

"In God's eyes none of us are ugly," her husband said. "Weren't we taught as kids that beauty is as beauty does? Didn't our parents try to teach us that true beauty is on the inside?"

You may not be able to assure everyone of inward beauty, but it's there because each person is a special, unrepeatable miracle of God. A generation ago, people bandied around a saying, "God don't make no junk." Maybe it's time to say, "God doesn't make ugly."

Why shouldn't we say that? It's true.

Perfect God, help my friends realize that each of them is beautiful in your eyes. You created them to glorify you. Even when their outer bodies waste away, remind them that the inner beauty is still there.

Amen.

9

"I Feel Guilty"

"I should visit him more often."

"I should have been kinder yesterday."

"Am I doing enough?"

"He complains and complains and then I lose my patience. Afterward I feel bad because he's sick."

"I saw her at the mall a few weeks ago and she looked awful. I wanted to encourage her, but I didn't. In fact, I ducked into a store so she wouldn't see me. I've felt guilty about it ever since."

"I wanted to get someone to come in for a couple of hours," the wife said, "but I couldn't do it. If something happens while I'm gone, it will be my fault."

Some of those comments are irrational, but they're real. People are sometimes shocked that they have such feelings, but they're common.

Even if you could explain your feelings, they wouldn't go away. I've experienced some of those emotions myself. My wife and I cared for Shirley's older sister, Edith, a total of seven and a half years. In the beginning of the seventh year the doctors diagnosed her with colon cancer. She became so bad we couldn't care for her any longer, and

we placed her in a skilled nursing facility.

That's when guilt hit me. Shirley went to see her every day and spent at least an hour at the nursing home. I didn't go daily. Shirley tried to make me feel that I didn't need to go as often as she did. I probably didn't, but I still felt guilty.

At various times I thought back over all the ways I had failed Edith, and guilt consumed me. The guilt came and went. Sometimes it would be as simple as a comment from a friend that would make me feel I had failed to give her the best care. Did I do all I could for her? Should I have done more?

I learned during that period of time that I couldn't control my feelings, and that they come and go. They're not reality, but we seem to think that if we feel a certain way, then it's true. Here's a sentence I began to say to myself and I've passed it on to others: "My negative feelings are emotions; they are not reality."

Simple words, but they are true.

Feeling guilty doesn't *make* me guilty. Feeling guilty means an emotion has attached itself to me. By repeating "My negative feelings are emotions; they are not reality," I slowly learned to distinguish between emotional reality and negative feelings.

That realization made me a better caregiver, and I was able to focus on the more positive things in life.

God, some days I struggle with guilt. I continually wonder if I have done everything I need to do. Remind me, loving Father, that my negative feelings are only emotions and not reality.

Amen.

10

When She Can Still Smell the Flowers

"I want people to send me flowers while I can smell them," Eunice Princic said to me several times before she died.

She didn't literally mean flowers, and she was a living example of giving flowers while people could appreciate them. She tried to find ways to encourage others and to help them to enjoy their lives. She tried to make them feel loved and valued as a person. She believed that giving bouquets was a vital part of her purpose. She was human like the rest of us, but she tried to show others appreciation and affirmation for who they were.

What better time to apply that idea than when someone we love has cancer? It doesn't matter whether that person will completely recover, go into remission, or be classified as terminal. No one is ever appreciated enough.

Why not give flowers to your loved ones every day? The flower could be a cheery note that says "I love you" or "Thank you for being my friend." How about sending a CD of the person's favorite music? Why not enlist others who love the person with cancer and ask them to send their own kind of flowers?

One woman learned to make greeting cards on her computer, so she made a card every week for her neighbor with breast cancer. "I tried to be creative and make it

No one is ever appreciated enough.

different every time. On one card I might copy an inspirational verse. On another it was a quotation I had read and liked. Sometimes I made it a simple expression of my love. She had been my neighbor for fifteen years, so we have a long history."

I heard of a man who loved red maple trees. As a boy in Maine, they surrounded his yard. When he was seriously ill with pancreatic cancer, his neighbor planted a red maple in the middle of the man's front yard. Every morning the sick man could see the maple. He watched the flowers form in the spring, and the leaves turned to a glowing red just before he died.

He loved that maple and made a little game of talking to the tree in the early mornings. "It gives me such peace to see you standing guard outside my window," he would often say.

Don't wait for the funeral! Let's give flowers now. The universe is filled with them—real, garden-grown flowers, pretty ones from the florists, or something more tangible and lasting, a simple testament of your love and care.

Creator God and Creative God, help me see the flowers in life and give them regularly to my loved one. It takes so little to hand out a flower of love and appreciation. Remind me that those flowers can make the difference in the quality of my loved one's day.

Amen.

Appendix

Practical Things You Can Do to Help Those Diagnosed with Cancer

Before You Offer Help

- Commit yourself to be an ongoing friend throughout the entire cancer process.

- Remind yourself that the diagnosis of serious illness changes people— even before their treatment begins.

- You don't know what's best for anyone with cancer. The best way to find out is to help them discover what they need.

- Make certain you're comfortable talking about the disease.

- Read and inquire about the disease. (The Internet and your local library can provide an abundance of information about every form of cancer.)

- Determine to stay positive no matter how negative the ill person sounds.

- Accept *their* feelings no matter how *you* feel. If they're pessimistic or discouraged, don't try to talk them out of their feelings.

- Prepare yourself that some people may not express their emotions easily. Accept them as they are.

- Some people may lash out in anger at God. You don't need to defend God or answer their anger. Focus on their pain and confusion.

- People handle problems differently. Cancer patients respond in the way most natural to their personality. Accept that.

- Promise yourself not to say:
  —"You must be strong."
  —"You should count your blessings."
  —"This was God's will."

- Begin to pray daily for the cancer patients you will visit.

- There is no one way to help. Discover the way most natural for you. (Some individuals are vocal; others are huggers. Some prefer to let others direct the conversation.)

- Use each experience as an opportunity to learn more about yourself.

What You Can Do Now

- Don't ask, "How are you?" Ask, "Do you feel like talking?"

- If the person is in pain, keep the visit short.

- Don't say, "Let me know if you need anything." (They probably won't and may not even know what they need.)

- Don't say, "I know how you feel." (You don't.)

- Don't treat them as invalids unless they are invalids.

- Let them talk as much or as little about their diagnosis and their prognosis as they choose. Don't push them.

- Don't tell them horror stories. ("My uncle had the same thing, and he died six months later.")

- Don't try to comfort them by describing how badly you or someone else suffered during surgery, radiation, or chemotherapy.

- If they speak out of unrealistic optimism, your role isn't to show them the mirror of reality.

- Be slow to offer advice, even if you're asked for it.

- Pray for the person every day. Say, "I've made a commitment to pray for you for (time period)."

- Before you pray, ask, "How would you like me to pray?" (Some may want you to pray for healing, others will ask for peace, and still others may ask you to pray for God's will. Respect their requests.)

- Pray with them. If appropriate, hold their hand or touch a shoulder. The human touch is powerful, and it shows the human connection.

- If appropriate, hug them.

- Be willing to sit silently with the person.

- Don't be afraid of the word "cancer" or "tumor." If you're afraid to use such words, the person may sense your discomfort and hold back.

- Allow the person to cry. Many people get nervous when someone around them becomes emotional, so be prepared to accept and to respect their actions. Crying is a great stress reliever. Think of crying as a step toward facing their disease.

- If you need to cry, don't hold back your tears.

- Offer to gather more information. Do research. Don't push the person to try alternative medicine or to find another doctor. If the patient asks for that kind of help, however, be willing to provide information or refer them to someone who can.

- Only if you're the appropriate person, talk to them about living wills, a legal power of attorney, and a medical power of attorney.

- Offer to drive the person for chemotherapy or radiation treatments (or arrange for others to do that).

- Depending on the seriousness of the cancer patient's condition, offer to do practical things, such as clean the house, assist in answering letters, cut the grass, or make phone calls.

- If the person with cancer knows it's terminal, help to plan a family reunion. Make it a time when people can lovingly say goodbye. Ask those who can't attend the event to write a letter to express their love.

- Help plan for a family picture with as many relatives and close friends as possible.

Long-Term Caregiving

- Let the seriousness of the disease determine the amount of time and commitment you offer.

- Help the sufferers find as many ways as possible to face the new phase in their lives.

- Don't be afraid to discuss the progress of the disease.

- Don't give false hope, but don't discourage.

- If possible, help them stand back and look objectively at what they have gone through.

   Ask such questions as:
   —"What have you discovered about yourself through this experience?"
   —"What have you learned about relationships?"
   —"In what ways do you now see the world differently?"
   —"How has your faith in God changed?"

- Encourage the person to join a support group for survivors of their type of cancer.

- Be willing to listen to their worries and concerns, especially, "Will my cancer recur?" (You don't have to provide an answer. Just listen.)

- Think about tangible things you can do that say, "I care."

- Plan celebrations for every anniversary of being cancer free.

- Plan a big party if the person passes the five-year mark.

In perplexities—when we cannot
tell what to do, when we
cannot understand
what is going on around us—
let us be calmed and
steadied and made patient
by the thought that what is hidden
from us is not hidden
from Him.

Frances Ridley Havergal